MW00987379

100 AFFIRMATIONS FOR SOBRIETY

POSITIVE SELF TALK FOR THOSE IN RECOVERY

APRYL HALL

PUBLISHED BY APRYL HALL

Introduction

On a desperate February morning in 2019, I awoke, felt the hangover before my eyes even opened, and wanted to end my life right then. Fortunately, I googled "rehab near me" instead and sought help for years of depression and prescription drug abuse coupled with more recent alcohol abuse. I've openly shared my story on social media, and this book is an attempt to take the gifts from sobriety and pass them along to others.

I consider affirmations a form of positive self-talk. They are mantras or statements I speak to myself. I often craft them to sound present-based, or in the direction I want to go. So instead of saying, "I want to," or "I will," I say, "I **am**." To craft your own affirmations, download the worksheet at

https://affirmations.phonesites.com/resourcelist

I'd done meditations with spoken affirmations and owned several books with affirmations. However, I hadn't yet incorporated them as a practice until recently. Honestly, I kinda thought they were silly. But then I started using affirmations in early 2021.

It wasn't until I began working on a book for a well-respected businessman that I really paid attention to the power of affirmations in creating the right mindset. Affirmations are not just a positive attitude (often used to describe affirmations) but a way to focus on my growth *as a person*. This gentleman incorporates affirmations into each chapter of his book, and he also convinced me to add a daily affirmation to my Morning Mindset writing prompts. So now, I write an affirmation each morning and see it on my calendar as I go through my day.

Affirmations have slowly transformed me. They help me stay focused and upbeat (two of my biggest problems). Using them has also helped me maintain sobriety. These short sentences read/spoken several times during a single day remind me how powerful I am. They also remind me of what I'm capable of in the future. I've turned my life in a new direction since the hopeless February morning, and it all started with my thoughts and changing my mind.

That practice of writing affirmations each day prompted me to create the book you're reading today. Writing this book to share with others has not only helped me stay sober during times I wanted to give up but also reminded me why I needed to *get* sober. Before sobriety, I'd wake up doing ok. But, by 6 pm, I'd given up all hope for myself and my situation. No matter how positive I started my days, I was down and out by the afternoon and looking forward to going out.

I'd have a drink in front of me to wash benzos down my throat. By nightfall, I'd have hit harder drugs, and my bar tab was climbing. I'd escaped my feelings, but I'd created more problems. If you know that feeling as well, I hope this small book helps you as much as practicing these principles did for me.

How to Use Affirmations

If you are not familiar with affirmations, most folks agree speaking them out loud is best. I prefer to write mine because I am a visual learner. Try both and see what works best for you.

Affirmations are not magic. They should be one of *many* tools at your disposal. I like the gentle reminder that I can succeed that reading or repeating an affirmation gives me throughout the day. I feel more confident when using them. Hence, repetition is a key component of using affirmations. We all have neural pathways in our brains that allow us to act, think, and feel. Once upon a time, it was believed that those pathways were hardwired for good at a certain point in life and could not change. Now scientists know otherwise.

The ability to rewire the brain and change those pathways is called neuroplasticity. For those who battled *any* kind of addiction (and that's almost everyone), your brain adapted to active addiction. The brain can also use that power to change again for the better. You **can** change your mind and change your life.

The brain also has a tendency to be fuzzy when determining if something is fact or imagination. Studies show that by using affirmations and positive mental images, your brain thinks it is *actually* experiencing those things. [1] This can be a good thing, especially when the images you create are associated with a positive change you seek.

I highly recommend the book *Unf#ck Your Brain* by Faith G. Harper, PhD, LPC-S, ACS, ACN. Her book is comprehensive but easy to digest. She goes into detail on how our brains work and how to rewire it. The chapter on addiction is fascinating. Without spoilers, Dr. Harper talks about addiction becoming our primary relationship. I related to that. And, I'd never framed my struggle that way. I wouldn't have admitted that drugs and alcohol were my #1 relationship before the day I asked for help, but my behavior said otherwise.

Breaking up with addiction is a process and requires many tools. Saying affirmations are just one way to help you (and your brain) take on new truths during the healing journey. Dr. Harper mentions prayer in her book as a coping skill. I view affirmations as a form of prayer. I will copy her words because they are perfect:

"What does prayer have to do with it? You may be rolling your eyes up in your head at me over this one, I know. Prayer? I don't do religious. But what we have, as a culture, agreed to call prayer is just **talking to**. Speaking to ourselves or something bigger than ourselves about our wants, needs, desires, and intentions. Remember the storytelling brain? Prayer is a natural mechanism of the storytelling brain. Talking through our situation in this manner can be far more powerful than talking to a friend, family member, or a therapist. It's a grounding experience that helps us be more aware of our thoughts, feelings, and behaviors."

As I mentioned, I recently added affirmations to my daily planner. As I look at my calendar, I am reminded of something positive and powerful. It's made a huge difference in my mood and attitude, and I encourage you to write and/or say your affirmations daily. I'm a kinesthetic and visual learner so writing my affirmations works. You may prefer the sound and speaking affirmations may help you more. Do whatever works for you.

You can scroll through these affirmations and find the ones that resonate with you to use. As with all other materials, leave anything that doesn't suit you at the curb. If one seems to suit you, use it once or every day. The choice is yours on how you use these affirmations.

You may also benefit from visiting Louise Hay's website
https://www.louisehay.com/affirmations/

I encourage you to create your own affirmations in your own tone and use words that may resonate more deeply with you.

1.
https://www.ncbi.nlm.nih.gov/pmc/articles/PMC4814782/

AFFIRMATIONS FOR SOBRIETY

My mess is now my message; whether I share my story or not, my path shows others what is possible.

I accept myself just as I am today. I am human, I have flaws, and that is totally acceptable to me because I am always improving.

I release any negative thoughts or resentments to my higher power. God refills my cup with love.

I am worthy and deserving of every dream in my heart.

I have hope in my heart and deliver it to others wherever I go.

Self-care is not selfish. I make time to relax, learn, sleep, play, and work to balance my life.

My past is one small chapter in an enormous book, and I'm the author. I choose what direction to take for my future.

I have a grand and unique purpose for being alive today.

I embrace every part of my story. Everything has happened FOR me.

I accept all people, places, things, and situations just as they are. By accepting them as they are, I also realize I can change my thoughts and actions. As a result, these things no longer disturb me.

I let go of the shit I cannot control. I stop ruminating and take control of my thoughts and actions.

The same spirit that raised the dead, heals the sick and performs miracles lives inside me.

I don't entertain thoughts that do not serve my higher self. I recognize these thoughts when they enter my mind. I no longer seek to numb them. Instead, I identify them and challenge the thoughts that cause me harm.

I recognize when my thinking is "all or nothing" and pause so I can bring more rational thoughts to my mind.

Nothing in life is ALWAYS one way or another. I stop catastrophic thinking. I accept the changes that come my way with grace and readiness.

I am not afraid of failure. I am a master at a comeback!

My life does not have to be perfect to be awesome.

I forgive everyone for everything. This releases ME from being tied to people who have hurt me. Forgiveness is a gift I give to myself; it doesn't excuse someone else's behavior.

Today I will proactively find happiness in the smallest pleasures—having water to drink, food to eat, a smile on my face, and everything I can see in this magnificent world.

My experiences make me a very tolerant person. I accept faults in others because I fully accept my own.

I have individual gifts to offer the world today that only I can give. I am deeply fulfilled and spread prosperity wherever I go.

I know I am strong and capable of achieving my goals. I know this is a truth deep in my soul. No one has to tell me this because I know it is so.

Yesterday is over, and I do not offer it space in my mind today. Instead, I am looking forward to my future and making the best of the present moment.

I have a servant's heart because I know firsthand what it feels like to struggle.

I am never alone. I am always walking alongside my higher power on this journey.

I take time to find healthy coping skills and my hidden talents every day.

I am not broken. I am a whole person, and I'm not fundamentally flawed. I'm human, and I am allowed to make mistakes. I will give myself plenty of grace today.

I have a community of supportive friends who all want me to succeed. They are always there for me and cheering me on even when I can't see or hear them.

I let go of the notion of perfection. Instead, I try to better myself every day and make progress every single day.

I am capable of accomplishing great things. Today, I remind myself that I can and will do whatever it takes to succeed today.

I focus on the positive stuff to protect my mental health and let the negative things go. I don't hold onto resentment and pain.

I take good care of myself mentally, spiritually, and physically.

I am a winner in every area of life. I don't need validation from others because I am comfortable in my own skin.

The trauma I have experienced is valid. I heal so that I no longer have a desire to cope in harmful ways.

I'm a fighter and a champ. When I look in the mirror, I see someone I am proud of.

I don't have to have it all together to be amazing. I'm a total badass right here, right now.

Today, I will do one small thing that brings me joy. It might include singing a song, dancing by myself, painting my nails, telling a joke, loving my pet, or cooking a healthy meal. *[if none of this brings you joy, insert something you enjoy that is not harmful but makes you happy]*

I am not ashamed of who I am because
I always learn valuable lessons and then
make better choices.

I am a very capable and resourceful
person. I am worthy of love and
belonging.

I am open to receiving the ample and
tremendous gifts that life has to offer. I
enjoy the little things that make every
day beautiful.

I expect miracles because I am one.

I control my thoughts and emotions instead of letting them control me.

My emotions are just a signal to my brain. I don't have to act on them or accept feelings as facts.

I close my eyes and take a deep breath when I am overwhelmed. I calm myself

down and clear my mind to ease any
pain or unrest I feel.

I take full ownership of my life. I
exceed my expectations with new ways
of thinking, coping, and feeling.

I no longer feel shame or guilt. Those
feelings do not serve me, and I stop the
self-sabotage they create in my life.

I love my body. It's the carriage for my
soul, and it requires daily maintenance.
I rest it, feed it, and protect it properly.

I look in the mirror and like the body I see.

I live with intention. I have greater meaning and purpose in my life than ever before. I direct my steps toward fulfilling a divine purpose today.

I know I can be of service to others as I go through this day.

I openly receive spiritual guidance from my higher power in order to reach my true potential.

I am strong! I remind myself of this throughout the day.

I am a creature of good habits. I make good choices.

I can feel love all around me, even when I cannot see it.

I am on a strict mental diet of positivity, optimism, forgiveness, acceptance, and gratitude.

I am thankful for all parts of my life, past and present.

I am grateful for my experiences, what I have learned from them, and how they have helped others to heal.

I know that what I think informs my beliefs, and beliefs determine my actions. Therefore, I carefully monitor my own thoughts, ideas, and actions today.

I don't dwell upon the past or engage in negative thinking about the past. I focus on what is within my control today.

I have the superpower to change my life and do incredible things.

The tone inside my head when I speak to myself is encouraging and compassionate. I am a champion, and I remind myself of this often.

I have the power to change my mind or my environment to protect myself.

I embrace change. I handle it like a pro. I can go with the flow and stay steadfast in positive thoughts. I've changed before, and I will again.

I can discern between thoughts that are part of old conditioned thinking and those that will benefit my new sober life.

I control my mind and my thoughts.
It's the greatest power on earth to
have self-control, and I am doing an
extraordinary job.

I create my own happiness, and I don't
rely on substances or other people to be
my source of contentment.

My mood is good because I control it
no matter what circumstances befall me
today.

Sobriety is my superpower. I may look like a regular person on the outside, but I am the hero of my life.

I am always learning new things about myself, and I can change anything I do not like.

I speak calmly and rationally to others without losing my temper.

I am an excellent communicator. I'm not overly aggressive or too passive.

I am good-spirited and a mentor to others.

I value and respect myself. I value and respect my body, my mind, and my spirit. Today I commit to one action that will improve my life.

I am a kind person and offer support to those who need it without compromising my own safety.

Today I keep my thoughts constructive, kind, optimistic, and positive.

I take 100% responsibility for my healing. Only I have the power to change my life. I seek help if I need it because I am courageous.

If I feel overwhelmed, I take a deep breath & focus on my heartbeat or my breath. This helps me stay grounded and avoid any thoughts that could lead to relapse.

I reach for healthy ways of coping with life. I incorporate daily habits that work

FOR me, not against me. I make time to nourish my mind, body, and soul.

I know that cravings are my brain's old way of coping. If I do experience a craving, I can pause and remind myself of my healthy coping practices.

By choosing new thoughts and ways to live, I am physically rewiring my brain for the better. Soon, the old habits will no longer be part of my toolbox.

I am grounded in the present moment. I do not worry, plan, or forecast—because I realize this is an ever-changing world. I can handle whatever comes my way without negative coping habits.

I forgive myself for turning to harmful coping mechanisms for survival in my past, and I make better choices today.

I improve my life every single day. I deserve the best life. I am worthy of loving relationships and achieving my goals.

My feelings may be strong, but I know they will pass. I am a survivor. I will not react to my emotions by using drugs or alcohol. This feeling is not permanent, and it leaves quickly.

I have hobbies and activities that are healthy for me. I avoid situations, places, and people who do not serve me.

I stay out of drama and petty matters that aren't healthy for me. I take great care of myself and place boundaries around anything or anyone who threatens my mental health.

I am not defined by my past because I am too busy improving my own life and others.

I keep myself safe. I protect my mental health. I have the courage to leave situations that are not healthy and not serving my higher good.

I am not defined by my addiction. I am worthy and deserving of love. I am constantly growing & bettering myself.

I healthily deal with my emotions. I have new coping skills to use when I need them, and it feels fantastic.

I am not easily triggered or panicked. Instead, I recognize what happens and practice my coping skills when in fight or flight mode.

I understand that people will not always appreciate my transformation, and I am ok with that. I will continue to focus on making myself better.

I have the best support system. I know they are cheering for me whether or not I can see and speak to them at this moment.

I do not need approval from others. I focus on doing the best I can so I always improve and can be of service.

I fail *forward*. I learn from every lesson and keep working toward the goals I have for my future.

I can learn anything. I am resourceful. If I don't know something, I can go find it. I have endless ways to grow my mind and develop myself.

I am committed to becoming the person I know I can be. I have a vision in my mind of my life in the future. It is bright. I am accomplished and clean. I am loved. I am safe.

I am capable of greatness, and I will properly focus my thoughts today to achieve it.

I create happiness in my life. My thoughts, beliefs, words, and actions create my reality. Therefore, I am dedicated to maintaining my thoughts, beliefs, words, and actions to be rewarded with happiness.

I am needed, worthy, loved, and I exceed expectations. Not just today, but every day. I play an important part in this universe, and I am so grateful to be sober and clean today.

I avoid all places, situations, and people who may cause me to relapse. I have a plan to avoid these things so I am not tempted to use them. Then, I follow through with my plans whenever I need to.

I have the tools I need to cope with life. I no longer get overwhelmed by my feelings.

I have gratitude for the small moments in everyday life. I know life is a one-way ticket. So I will not go back to addiction and cause further pain. I know the small moments make my life amazing, and I look forward to them today with optimism.

I do something every day to promote my spiritual growth. Spiritual growth is a deeply personal issue, and I cannot do it wrong. A healthy spiritual practice keeps my mind calm.

I have faith that is unshakable. I let go of *my* way and trust God's way.

THE END

Made in the USA
Las Vegas, NV
16 October 2023

79180778R00026